HOTEL
INSOMNIA

Charles Simic

OTHER BOOKS BY CHARLES SIMIC

HOTEL
INSOMNIA

CHARLES
SIMIC

A Harvest / HBJ Original

Harcourt Brace Jovanovich, Publishers

San Diego   New York   London

HBJ

Requests for permission to make copies of any part of the work should be mailed to: Permissions Department, Harcourt Brace Jovanovich, Publishers, 8th Floor, Orlando, Florida 32887.

Some of these poems first appeared, often in different versions, in the following magazines, to whose editors a grateful acknowledgment is made: *APR, Arete, Boulevard, The Gettysburg Review, Grand Street, The Kenyon Review, Michigan Quarterly Review, New Directions Annual, The New Yorker, The New York Times, The Paris Review, Ploughshares, Poetry, Raritan, River City,* and *Vox.*

Library of Congress Cataloging-in-Publication Data
Simic, Charles, 1938–
     Hotel insomnia: poems/by Charles Simic.—1st ed.
        p.   cm.
     ISBN 0-15-142188-9
     ISBN 0-15-642182-8 (pbk.)
     1. Title.
    PS3569.I4725H68   1992
811'.54—dc20   91-44897

Designed by Lydia D'moch
Printed in the United States of America
First edition
A B C D E

for Helen, Philip, and Nicky

CONTENTS

ONE

TWO

THREE

ONE

EVENING CHESS

The Black Queen raised high
In my father's angry hand.

THE CONGRESS OF THE INSOMNIACS

Mother of God, everyone is invited:
Stargazing Peruvian shepherds,
Old men on sidewalks of New York.
You, too, doll with eyes open
Listening to the rain next to a sleeping child.

A big hotel ballroom with mirrors on every side.
Think about it as you lie in the dark.
Angels on its ornate ceilings,
Naked nymphs in what must be paradise.

There's a stage, a lectern,
An usher with a flashlight.
Someone will address this gathering yet
From his bed of nails.
Sleeplessness is like metaphysics.
Be there.

MATCHES

Very dark when I step
On the street
But then he shows up
The one who plays with matches
In my dreams

I have never seen
His face his eyes

Why do I always
Have to be so slow
And the matches already
Down to his fingertips

If it's a house
Time only for a glimpse
If a woman—
Just a single kiss
Before the shadows converge

I could be dining
Making a snowball
Having my teeth pulled
By the Pope in Rome
Or running naked
Over a battlefield

The one with matches
Knows and won't say

He likes only abandoned games
Illegible cities
Great loves that go out
In a puff

THE CITY

At least one crucified at every corner.
The eyes of a mystic, madman, murderer.
They know it's truly for nothing.
The eyes do. All the martyr's sufferings
On parade. Exalted mother of us all
Tending her bundles on the sidewalk,
Speaking to each as if it were a holy child.

There were many who saw none of this.
A couple lingered on kissing lustily
Right where someone lay under a newspaper.
His bloody feet, swollen twice their size,
Jutted out into the cold of the day,
Grim proofs of a new doctrine.

I tell you, I was afraid. A man screamed
And continued walking as if nothing had happened.
Everyone whose eyes I sought avoided mine.
Was I beginning to resemble him a little?
I had no answer to any of these questions.
Neither did the crucified on the next corner.

THE INFINITE

On a long shot, I went searching
For you Miranda, downtown
When the offices empty at five,
Knowing neither the building nor the street.
I had my lust to lead me
With its sleepwalker's stride.

The city, that winter evening,
Like an opera house on fire.
Hundreds of fleeing faces to examine,
Hundreds of false sightings to pursue,
Only to overtake a complete stranger,

Someone spooked by what my eyes told her,
Someone equally ethereal,
Already lost in the crowd,
Already replaced by someone new.
Until she, too, vanished.

One lone wino left behind berating God.
The store windows brightly lit
With their naked, all-smiling dummies.
The hour ruled by destiny,
Auspicious to chance meetings.

"I was working late," you'd say.
"If I'm dressed in black, it's because
I went to a funeral of a friend."

We'd be voluptuously alone
On a street of tall and dark buildings.
The grand parade of clouds
And the moon above us—
With love screaming bloody murder!

OBSCURE BEGINNINGS

I was a winter fly on the ceiling
In the house of arachnids.
Silence reigned. Queen Insomnia
Sipped tea in the parlor,
Death and Judgment by her side.

The ceiling a polar expedition.
The window a theater of cruelty
With its view of the pretty meadow:
Sheep nibbling wildflowers,
And the sky beyond them vast and empty.

Death notices posted in every room.
The old woman dressing a small child for slaughter
In a convent's school uniform.
The ceiling pale as the flowers.
The red parrot screaming in the parrot house.

STUB OF A RED PENCIL

You were sharpened to a fine point
With a rusty razor blade.
Then the unknown hand swept the shavings
Into its moist palm
And disappeared from view.

You lay on the desk next to
The official-looking document
With a long list of names.
It was up to us to imagine the rest:
The high ceiling with its cracks
And odd-shaped water stains;
The window with its view
Of roofs covered with snow.

An inconceivable, varied world
Surrounding your severe presence
On every side,
Stub of a red pencil.

THE PRODIGAL

Dark morning rain
Meant to fall
On a prison and a school yard,
Falling meanwhile
On my mother and her old dog.

How slow she shuffles now
In my father's Sunday shoes.
The dog by her side
Trembling with each step
As he tries to keep up.

I am on another corner waiting
With my head shaved.
My mind hops like a sparrow
In the rain.
I'm always watching and worrying about her.

Everything is a magic ritual,
A secret cinema,
The way she appears in a window hours later
To set the empty bowl
And spoon on the table,
And then exits
So that the day may pass,
And the night may fall

Into the empty bowl,
Empty room, empty house,
While the rain keeps
Knocking at the front door.

HOTEL INSOMNIA

I liked my little hole,
Its window facing a brick wall.
Next door there was a piano.
A few evenings a month
A crippled old man came to play
"My Blue Heaven."

Mostly, though, it was quiet.
Each room with its spider in heavy overcoat
Catching his fly with a web
Of cigarette smoke and revery.
So dark,
I could not see my face in the shaving mirror.

At 5 A.M. the sound of bare feet upstairs.
The "Gypsy" fortuneteller,
Whose storefront is on the corner,
Going to pee after a night of love.
Once, too, the sound of a child sobbing.
So near it was, I thought
For a moment, I was sobbing myself.

TRAGIC ARCHITECTURE

School, prison, trees in the wind,
I climbed your gloomy stairs,
Stood in your farthest corners
With my face to the wall.

The murderer sat in the front row.
A mad little Ophelia
Wrote today's date on the blackboard.
The executioner was my best friend.
He already wore black.
The janitor brought us mice to play with.

In that room with its red sunsets—
It was eternity's time to speak,
So we listened
As if our hearts were made of stone.

All of that in ruins now.
Cracked, peeling walls
With every window broken.
Not even a naked light bulb left
For the prisoner forgotten in solitary,
And the school boy left behind
Watching the bare winter trees
Lashed by the driving wind.

MAKERS OF LABYRINTHS

I must be absolutely alone when I think,
And on the highest parapet
Overlooking the empty street.
The dusty store window down below
Is full of phantoms at sunset.

There goes my old man. He is already
    the age I am now.
With eyes closed
He calls the waiters by their secret names:
St. Isaac, the Syrian,
St. Nilus, who wrote on prayer.
The wine of eternal ambiguities,
If you please, to the health of the crow
Sitting on the top of a white church.

His life, too, is a fantastic maze.
Our misfortunes are builders.
They always forget about windows,
Make the ceilings low and heavy.
"It's only a paper moon," they sing . . .
But I'm getting ahead of myself.

At the end of a dark corridor
There is a lit match in a trembling hand
"I still have stage fright,"
The beautiful woman says,
And then she leads us past wardrobes
With mirrors and creaking doors

Where whispering dresses hang,
Whispering corsets, button shoes—
The kind you'd wear while riding a goat.

Her daughter, we are told, is consumptive.
There's a sign of death's greasy thumbprint
On her angelic face.
She wants me to play under the table
Of the silent card players.

We play and it's like the palace at Knossos.
Memory, my heart's only burnt match:
Her hand guiding me in the ruins,
And the cards whispering over our heads
Made giddy by our youth and our love.

THE INANIMATE OBJECT

In my long late night talks with the jailers, I raised again the question of the object: Does it remain indifferent whether it is perceived or not? (I had in mind the one concealed and found posthumously while the newly vacated cell was fumigated and swept.)

"Like a carved-wood demon of some nightmarish species," said one. "In cipher writ," said another. We were drinking a homemade brew that made our heads spin. "When a neck button falls on the floor and hardly makes a sound," said the third with a smile, but I said nothing.

"If only one could leave behind a little something to make others stop and think," I thought to myself.

In the meantime, there was my piece of broken bottle to worry about. It was green and had a deadly cutting edge. I no longer remembered its hiding place, unless I had only dreamed of it, or this was another cell, another prison in an infinite series of prisons and long night talks with my jailers.

OUTSIDE BIAGGI'S FUNERAL HOME

Three old women sat knitting
On the sidewalk
Every time I walked by.
Good evening ladies,
I'd say,
Good morning, too,
What a lovely time of year
To be alive.

While they stared at me,
The way the deaf stare
In a school they go to,
The deaf and dumb.
Two of them resuming their knitting,
The third watching me
Go my way
With her mouth open.

And that was all.
I left town and they stayed
Knitting away.
They could be still there today
For it's that kind of day,
Sweet and mild,
I thought of them again
After a long, long while.

THE TIGER

in memory of George Oppen

In San Francisco, that winter,
There was a dark little store
Full of sleepy Buddhas.
The afternoon I walked in,
No one came out to greet me.
I stood among the sages
As if trying to read their thoughts.

One was huge and made of stone.
A few were the size of a child's head
And had stains the color of dried blood.
There were even some no bigger than mice,
And they appeared to be listening.

"The winds of March, black winds,
The gritty winds," the dead poet wrote.

At sundown his street was empty
Except for my long shadow
Open before me like scissors.
There was his house where I told the story
Of the Russian soldier,
The one who looked Chinese.

He lay wounded in my father's bed,
And I brought him water and matches.

For that he gave me a little tiger
Made of ivory. Its mouth was open in anger,
But it had no stripes left.

There was the night when I colored
Its eyes black, its tongue red.
My mother held the lamp for me,
While worrying about the kind of luck
This beast might bring us.

The tiger in my hand growled faintly
When we were alone in the dark,
But when I put my ear to the poet's door
That afternoon, I heard nothing.

"The winds of march, black winds,
The gritty winds," he once wrote.

MISS NOSTRADAMUS

Once I adored a seeress, a long-legged one. We roamed the streets of New York like dreamy newlyweds trailing a funeral of some lofty vision.

"It's like glimpsing the world's secret among the empty aquariums and bird cages in the back of a dime store," she told me between kisses.

And then late one night, with eyes veiled as the sirens sounded:

"Overcoats thrown over their pajamas, the lovers of tragedies now stand in ecstasy, there where a naked babe is being thrown out of a high window by a woman in flames."

PLACE AT THE OUTSKIRTS

Gods trying different costumes
In the kitchen of a darkened restaurant,
Then emerging one by one
To serve you.

For the moment, just a glass of red wine
At the table with a view of the empty street,
A row of abandoned buildings,
And the cloudless evening sky.

The philosopher in you says:
The world is a beautiful idea.
Aphrodite with arms missing dressed as a nun
Waiting to take your order.

CLOUDS GATHERING

It seemed the kind of life we wanted.
Wild strawberries and cream in the morning.
Sunlight in every room.
The two of us walking by the sea naked.

Some evenings, however, we found ourselves
Unsure of what comes next.
Like tragic actors in a theater on fire,
With birds circling over our heads,
The dark pines strangely still,
Each rock we stepped on bloodied by the sunset.

We were back on our terrace sipping wine.
Why always this hint of an unhappy ending?
Clouds of almost human appearance
Gathering on the horizon, but the rest lovely
With the air so mild and the sea untroubled.

The night suddenly upon us, a starless night.
You lighting a candle, carrying it naked
Into our bedroom and blowing it out quickly.
The dark pines and grasses strangely still.

TWO

FOLK SONGS

Sausage-makers of History,
The bloody kind,
You all hail from a village
Where the dog barking at the moon
Is the only poet.

*

O King Oedipus, O Hamlet,
Fallen like flies
In the pot of cabbage soup,
No use beating with your fists,
Or sticking your tongues out.

*

Christ-faced spider on the wall
Darkened by evening shadows,
I spent my childhood on a cross
In a yard full of weeds,
White butterflies, and white chickens.

WAR

The trembling finger of a woman
Goes down the list of casualties
On the evening of the first snow.

The house is cold and the list is long.

All our names are included.

A BOOK FULL OF PICTURES

Father studied theology through the mail
And this was exam time.
Mother knitted. I sat quietly with a book
Full of pictures. Night fell.
My hands grew cold touching the faces
Of dead kings and queens.

There was a black raincoat
      in the upstairs bedroom
Swaying from the ceiling,
But what was it doing there?
Mother's long needles made quick crosses.
They were black
Like the inside of my head just then.

The pages I turned sounded like wings.
"The soul is a bird," he once said.
In my book full of pictures
A battle raged: lances and swords
Made a kind of wintry forest
With my heart spiked and bleeding in its branches.

EVENING WALK

You give the appearance of listening
To my thoughts, O trees,
Bent over the road I am walking
On a late summer evening
When every one of you is a steep staircase
The night is slowly descending.

The high leaves like my mother's lips
Forever trembling, unable to decide,
For there's a bit of wind,
And it's like hearing voices,
Or a mouth full of muffled laughter,
A huge dark mouth we can all fit in
Suddenly covered by a hand.

Everything quiet. Light
Of some other evening strolling ahead,
Long-ago evening of silk dresses,
Bare feet, hair unpinned and falling.
Happy heart, what heavy steps you take
As you follow after them in the shadows.

The sky at the road's end cloudless and blue.
The night birds like children
Who won't come to dinner.
Lost children in the darkening woods.

HOTEL STARRY SKY

Millions of empty rooms with TV sets turned on.
I wasn't there yet I saw everything.
Titanic on the screen like a
    birthday cake sinking.
Poseidon, the night clerk, blew out the candles.

How much should we tip the blind bellboy?
At three in the morning the gum machine
    in the empty lobby
With its freshly cracked mirror
Is the new Madonna with her infant child.

CAGED FORTUNETELLER

Sleeplessness, you're like a pawnshop
Open late
On a street of failing businesses.
The owner plays a flute,
And it's like night birds calling
In a city where there are no birds.

There's a painting over the cash register:
Of a stiff Quaker couple dressed in black.
They each hold a cat under their arm.
One is a tiger, the other is Siamese.
The eyes are closed because it's very late,
And because cats see better with eyes closed.

The pawnshop owner has an electric fortuneteller
In a glass cage.
Now he plugs her in and turns the other lights off.
"O foolish fellow," says she,
"If you can find your way, please hurry to me,
I'll even take out my breasts at the door
To light your way in the dark."

The street is shadowy and so is the sky.
We could be meeting Jacob and the angel.
We could be meeting our sleeplessness,
And the nun who carries morphine to the dying,
The black nun in soft, furry slippers.

COUNTRY LUNCH

A feast in the time of plague—
That's the way it feels today:
This chicken and rice,
Sausage and shrimp on the table.

The festive company of flushed, dreamy faces
In the shade of a big old tree,
In the heat of the afternoon,
When the flies grow sluggish,
And the head begins to spin with wine,
The women bare their breasts,
The men sit naked to the waist.

Everyone suddenly so beautiful:
Even the girl lying on the ground
    with the dogs,
And shaking with laughter,
Whose nose has started to bleed.

TO THINK CLEARLY

What I need is a pig and an angel.
The pig to stick his nose in a slop bucket,
The angel to scratch his back
And say sweet things in his ear.

The pig knows what's in store for him.
Give him hope, angel child,
With that foreverness stuff.
Don't go admiring yourself
In the butcher's knife
As if it were a whore's mirror,
Or tease him with a blood-stained apron
By raising it above your knees.

The pig has stopped eating
And stands among us thinking.
Already the crest of the rooster blazes
In the morning darkness.
He's not crowing but his eyes are fierce
As he struts across the yard.

POEM

Those happy days when I climbed
The bare cemetery tree holding on to my life.
The evening clouds were the sea,
And I was the captain in the crow's nest.

It was an old cemetery.
Nobody got buried there anymore.
They lay squeezed like the poor in their beds,
And I was the captain in the crow's nest.

QUICK EATS

Trees like evangelists
On their rostrums,
Arms raised in blessing over the evening fields.

*

I saw that and more
Sitting by the open window
In the back room
Of Herman's Funeral Home.

*

Every leaf now, every bush
Helps the night
Darken and quiet the world.

*

Birds of a feather,
Friends of the blues,
Listen, pay attention.

*

What runs but never walks,
O Mother?
What goes out without putting its coat on?

*

Winding road, the place of vanishings . . .

I am the original nomad exquisite,
I am setting out astride my phantom Rocinante.

*

Imponderabilia, old-fashioned gal,
Strolling among the lengthening shadows,
I hear your ass was tattooed in Singapore.

*

It's this sly little wine I sip,
Chill with twilight.

Château Abracadabra.

*

No two rain drops,
No two blades of grass
Whisper your name alike.

*

QUICK EATS in blood-red neon,
Miles away
In the dark-clouded,
Storm-threatening West.

He happened to find himself on the stairs of a quiet building, checking the sky for rain through a dusty windowpane, when he caught sight of them out for a walk.

The father wore black down to his gloves and heavy shoes. She did too. They could have been in mourning except for the nasty stick he carried.

Father Time and daughter Truth, it occurred to him. The father already hurrying the pale girl behind some bushes in the park.

THE CHAIR

This chair was once a student of Euclid.

The book of his laws lay on its seat.
The schoolhouse windows were open,
So the wind turned the pages
Whispering the glorious proofs.

The sun set over the golden roofs.
Everywhere the shadows lengthened,
But Euclid kept quiet about that.

MISSING CHILD

You of the dusty, sun-yellowed picture
I saw twenty years ago
On the window of a dry-cleaning store.
I thought of you again tonight,
In this chilly room where I sat by the window
Watching the street,
As your mother must've done every night,

And still does, for all I know.
The sky dark and cloudy for us both.
A bit of rain beginning to fall
On the same old city, the same old street
With a padlocked, dimly-lit store,
And the growing horror of the truth
With its poster of a firemen's ball.

THE PUPPET SHOW

Quick Eats

The deaf and dumb waiter
Serving a piece of burnt toast
And a cup of black coffee
To a blind old woman

In M. with the night falling.

Heroic Age

Icarus wore bright red sneakers.
Jesus was a short-order cook.
Alexander the Great stood outside the
      horse players' hangout.
Ulysses was the name of a three-legged dog.

Puppet

The infinite number of lines
That join to me things and beings,
So that a diagram
Of any moment in my life
Looks like a child's scribble.

The Mystic Hour

God likes to dress himself as the devil
And walk these streets
Full of children at play.

Storefront Church

A scar-faced preacher
Was showing a used condom
To a feeble-minded boy.

A condom with spikes.

In the Night

The winds are making soup
For the insomniacs,

Weathervane soup.

MANY ZEROS

The teacher rises voiceless before a class
Of pale, tight-lipped children.
The blackboard behind him as black as the sky
Light-years from the earth.

It's the silence the teacher loves,
The taste of the infinite in it.
The stars like teeth marks on children's pencils.
Listen to it, he says happily.

TRUE HISTORY

Which cannot be put into words—
Like a fly on the map of the world
In the travel agent's window.

That street empty in the afternoon heat
Except for my old father
Pressing his head against the glass
To observe her better
As she drags her threadbare shadow
From New York to Shanghai.

He not sure whether to alert his friend,
The barber, napping next door
With a sheet draped over his head.

MARINA'S EPIC

The Eskimos were ravaging Peru.
Grandfather fought the Hittites.
Mother sold firecrackers to the Bedouins.

One night when the moon was full
She met the lion who ate Lev Tolstoy.

We were inmates of an orphanage in Cracow;
A prison in Panama;
A school for beggars in Genoa.

My sister insisted on rescuing ladybugs.
Down a succession of gloomy corridors
She carried the glistening and shivering creature
On the long nail of her index finger.

Our Fate was a crackpot inventor
Working in a garage.

In Paris I knew a Russian lady
Who scrubbed floors at the opera
With a rose between her teeth like Carmen.

Father played a dead man in a German movie.
It was silent. The piano player looked like
Edgar Allan Poe wearing a Moroccan fez.

We stood outside a pink motel in Arizona singing:
"We love you life
Even though you're always laughing at us."

The next day I joined the Tibetans.
They had a holy mountain
From which one could see Los Angeles.

Sardinian goat cheese, Greek olives,
    Hungarian sausage
On the table—
Because memory makes you hungry.

On the back of a sleeping shark
We sailed the stormy Atlantic
Taking turns to mend the rips in grandmother's
    wedding dress
We used as a sail.

In America the movie screens were as big
    as the pyramids.

Broadway was a river like the Amazon.
Drowned heads popping up with eyes open:
Ophelias and Valentinos by the thousands.

In Japan they were catching ghosts
With chopsticks.
In Amsterdam there was a Christmas tree
In a whorehouse.

I stood on the corner with the Zulus.
We were waiting for fool's bells,
Gypsy woman's love potion,
General Washington to ride by on his horse
And nod in our direction.

THREE

FIGURE IN THE LANDSCAPE

for Mark

The vision of heaven
Some early settler beheld
As he ventured inland over the mountains,
The sudden dreamlike river
And the valley on the other side,
Bounteous and lush
As if after a summer rain.

The story, I read somewhere,
Of how, while admiring the wilderness,
He was startled by
The solitary figure of a man,
Which, as he rubbed his eyes,
Vanished, so that he was left
Troubled, searching again
For that phantom speck
Among the trees and their shadows.

The distant hills and meadows lit
By the last rays of sunlight,
The woods already dark and mute.
Each shrub like another stranger,
Each leaf quieted by a hidden hand.
The grand spectacle of night
Opening its black wings in the New World
As if never to close them again.

AT THE VACANCY SIGN

Past the butcher
With pig's head in the window
And the stray dog
At his keyhole.

Past the sex shop.
The one awake
In a strange room,
Mouth open
Like a dead man,
Trying to remember
How he got there.

The one asking himself,
Was it the sunlight
On his face,
The silence of the house,
That huge spider
Next to the red stain
On the ceiling?

Dark suit,
Empty sleeves dangling
On a chair across the room.
The red necktie
Like a hangman's rope on fire.
Shoes like two crows
Grown old and wretched
Waiting for him to awake.

The single window
With a view of the sky
Cloudless and blue.
Day like secret happiness
In an imagined world,
Momentary, impermanent.

Windswept street
With its shuttered shops,
Its lengthening shadows,
High walls and closed doors.

Late afternoon sunlight
With one golden dead fly
On the table.
And the year unknown.
And the hour fugitive.

LOST GLOVE

Here's a woman's black glove.
It ought to mean something.
A thoughtful stranger left it
On the red mailbox at the corner.

Three days the sky was troubled,
Then today a few snowflakes fell
On the glove, which someone,
In the meantime, had turned over,
So that its fingers could close

A little . . . Not yet a fist.
So I waited, with the night coming.
Something told me not to move.
Here where flames rise from trash barrels,
And the homeless sleep standing up.

SPRING

This is what I saw—old snow on the ground,
Three blackbirds preening themselves,
And my neighbor stepping out in her nightdress
To hang her husband's shirts on the line.

The morning wind made them hard to pin.
It swept the dress so high above her knees,
She had to stop what she was doing
And have a good laugh, while covering herself.

STORY OF MY LUCK

There was a famous palm reader
Living on my street when I was a kid.
We all called him Count Dracula.
He took a peek into my palm once
And his mouth fell open.

A kind of mad scribble, he opined.
Love and fate crossed out viciously.
Body and soul shunning each other.
My death already consummated.
The blood-curdling shriek of my mother audible.

I've never seen a hand like yours,
He concluded, and stared at me,
Bug-eyed, letting the hand go finally,
While my friends tittered,
And all I could do was scratch my head.

LOVE WORKER

Diligent solely in what concerns love;
In all else dilatory, sleep-walking, sullen.
Some days you could not budge me
Even if you were to use a construction crane.
I work only at loving and being loved.
Tell me, people, ain't it right
To lie in bed past noon
Eating fried chicken and guzzling beer?

Consider the many evils thus avoided
While finding new places to kiss
        with greasy lips.
Easier for Schwarzkopf to take Kuwait
Than for us to draw the curtains.
The sky blue. It must be summer already.
The blind street preacher is shouting down below.
Your breasts and hair are flying—
Like the clouds, the white clouds.

ROMANTIC SONNET

Evenings of sovereign clarity—
Wine and bread on the table,
Mother praying,
Father naked in bed.

Was I that skinny boy stretched out
In the field behind the house,
His heart cut out with a toy knife?
Was I the crow hovering over him?

Happiness, you are the bright red lining
Of the dark winter coat
Grief wears inside out.

This is about myself when I'm remembering,
And your long insomniac's nails,
O Time, I keep chewing and chewing.

DANDELIONS

We were fabulously lucky.
We became dandelions.
Before we were even born
We kept wishing to be dandelions.
Next we found ourselves traveling
Out of the great unknown.
We rode down in a train
Sixteen coaches long,
We sat prim and proper
In our golden yellow dresses.
Others came as black widows,
Little monkeys, and red birds,
And of course many ants,
Snuggled together and looking glum.

SOME NIGHTS

Many fine pastries line the shelves
Of our town library. Miss Reese
Dips her finger here and there
While she walks the dim aisles
Looking for a certain book.

"I want something with truffles of Périgord,"
Is what I said to her.
"In Périgord where the poets only think of love,"
She exclaimed gaily,
Her mouth smeared with strawberry and cream.

I'm squeezing her hand; she is squeezing
My hand. We are going down
To the cellar where they keep
Little dark chocolates
Filled with almonds of heaven and hell.

BEAUTY

I'm telling you, this was the real thing, the same one they kicked out of Aesthetics, told her she didn't exist!

O you simple, indefinable, ineffable, and so forth. I like your black apron, and your new Chinese girl's hairdo. I also like naps in the afternoon, well-chilled white wine, and the squabbling of philosophers.

What joy and happiness you give us each time you reach over the counter to take our money, so we catch a whiff of your breath. You've been chewing on sesame crackers and garlic salami, divine creature!

When I heard the old man, Plotinus, say something about "every soul wanting to possess you," I gave him a dirty look, and rushed home to unwrap and kiss the pink ham you sliced for me with your own hand.

STREET SCENE

A blind little boy
With a paper sign
Pinned to his chest.
Too small to be out
Begging alone,
But there he was.

This strange century
With its slaughter of the innocent,
Its flight to the moon—
And now he waiting for me
In a strange city,
On a street where I lost my way.

Hearing me approach,
He took a rubber toy
Out of his mouth
As if to say something,
But then he didn't.

It was a head, a doll's head,
Badly chewed,
Held high for me to see.
The two of them grinning at me.

EARLY MORNING IN JULY

The streets were cool
After the heat of the night.
The dives, their doors open,
Smelled of stale beer.
Someone swept the floor
With even strokes.
He was pale as Confucius.
Martha Washington, her hair in a beehive,
Yawned in the glass booth
Of a movie theater.

Yesterday I saw Ulysses
Make Greek pastry.
Joan of Arc was at the dry cleaner's
Standing on a chair
With pins in her mouth.
St. Francis sold piranhas in a pet store.
At midnight Circe's daughters
Flew on a motorcycle.
Thomas Alva Edison
Roamed the streets in white socks
And blood on his shirt.

And now this sea breeze,
This unexpected coolness.
The small, sickly tree on your block
Hasn't grown much in years.
It shivers with happiness
With its few remaining leaves,

As if Emanuel Swedenborg
Was now whispering to the spirits
On Eighth Avenue.

MY QUARREL WITH THE INFINITE

I preferred the fleeting,
Like a memory of a sip of wine
Of noble vintage
On the tongue with eyes closed . . .

When you tapped me on the shoulder,
O light, unsayable in your splendor.
A lot of good you did to me.
You just made my insomnia last longer.

I sat rapt at the spectacle,
Secretly ruing the fugitive:
All its provisory, short-lived
Kisses and enchantments.

Here with the new day breaking,
And a single scarecrow on the horizon
Directing the traffic
Of crows and their shadows.

PYRAMIDS AND SPHINXES

There's a street in Paris
Called rue des Pyramides.
Once I imagined it was lined
With sand and pyramids.

The Sunday I went there to make sure,
A poor old woman with a limp
Overtook me without looking my way.
She could've been Egyptian
Because of her advanced age.

Leaning on a cane and still hurrying
Past the shuttered storefronts
As if there was a parade somewhere,
Or an execution to see—
A bloody head held high by its hair!

The day was cold. She soon disappeared,
While I studied a peeling circus poster
Under which there was another
With the head of a sphinx staring at me.

THE ABSENT SPIDER

There's its web, but I never saw a spider here,
Except for a fake one, the kind made from rubber
Sold in the back of a dime store
With fish bowl ornaments and bath toys.

We wanted a hairy spider to frighten Mary,
But instead bought her a rattlesnake.
It looked real. It looked positively deadly
With its forked tongue sticking out.

She screamed. She didn't think it was funny.
Her brother threw the snake high in the air.
It twisted and untwisted as if trying to fly.
A tree hooked it. We threw rocks but to no avail.

When winter came and the tree lost its leaves
We saw the snake shivering on the branch
As if it were cold. The spider stayed
    where it was
In the back of the dime store.

It was black. Even its eyes were.
The store had no customers at Christmas time.
The hundreds of cut-rate dolls on the shelves
Appeared astonished, pink and naked beyond belief.

THE ARTIST

Do you remember the crazy guy
Who stuck candles in his hat
So he could paint the sea at night?
Alone on that empty Jersey beach,
He kept squinting into the dark,
And waving his brush wildly.

Theresa said he got the dumb idea
From a movie she saw once.
Still, there he was, bearded and hairy
Like the devil himself
Piling one murky color on top of another
While we stood around watching,
The candles on his head flickering
Then going out one by one.

THE OLD WORLD

for Dan and Jeanne

I believe in the soul; so far
It hasn't made much difference.
I remember an afternoon in Sicily.
The ruins of some temple.
Columns fallen in the grass like naked lovers.

The olives and goat cheese tasted delicious
And so did the wine
With which I toasted the coming night,
The darting swallows,
The Saracen wind and moon.

It got darker. There was something
Long before there were words:
The evening meal of shepherds . . .
A fleeting whiteness among the trees . . .
Eternity eavesdropping on time.

The goddess going to bathe in the sea.
She must not be followed.
These rocks, these cypress trees,
May be her old lovers.
Oh to be one of them, the wine whispered to me.

COUNTRY FAIR

for Hayden Carruth

If you didn't see the six-legged dog,
It doesn't matter.
We did and he mostly lay in the corner.
As for the extra legs,

One got used to them quickly
And thought of other things.
Like, what a cold, dark night
To be out at the fair.

Then the keeper threw a stick
And the dog went after it
On four legs, the other two flapping behind,
Which made one girl shriek with laughter.

She was drunk and so was the man
Who kept kissing her neck.
The dog got the stick and looked back at us.
And that was the whole show.